YOUR KNOWLEDGE HAS VALUE

- We will publish your bachelor's and master's thesis, essays and papers

- Your own eBook and book - sold worldwide in all relevant shops

- Earn money with each sale

Upload your text at www.GRIN.com
and publish for free

Bibliographic information published by the German National Library:

The German National Library lists this publication in the National Bibliography; detailed bibliographic data are available on the Internet at http://dnb.dnb.de .

This book is copyright material and must not be copied, reproduced, transferred, distributed, leased, licensed or publicly performed or used in any way except as specifically permitted in writing by the publishers, as allowed under the terms and conditions under which it was purchased or as strictly permitted by applicable copyright law. Any unauthorized distribution or use of this text may be a direct infringement of the author s and publisher s rights and those responsible may be liable in law accordingly.

Imprint:

Copyright © 2015 GRIN Verlag, Open Publishing GmbH
Print and binding: Books on Demand GmbH, Norderstedt Germany
ISBN: 9783668560840

This book at GRIN:

http://www.grin.com/en/e-book/378293/enhanced-leadership-an-overview

Navid Bolorforoush

Enhanced Leadership. An Overview

GRIN Publishing

GRIN - Your knowledge has value

Since its foundation in 1998, GRIN has specialized in publishing academic texts by students, college teachers and other academics as e-book and printed book. The website www.grin.com is an ideal platform for presenting term papers, final papers, scientific essays, dissertations and specialist books.

Visit us on the internet:

http://www.grin.com/

http://www.facebook.com/grincom

http://www.twitter.com/grin_com

Leadership has been a topic of investigation for many decades due to competitive nature of the global economy and emergent prominence of corporate governance. The literature on the topic is abundant and wide range of existing studies can seem disjointed at times. However, over the past 80 years, leadership theories have seen four key generations: trait theories, behavioural, contingency and transformational theories. It is important to note that these theories are not merely exclusive or comprehensive on their own but follows a progressive pattern (Maurik, 2001). This means that there have been elements added or included from one generation to the next that link one to the other and the root can be traced back to sixteenth century in military history, major religions and politics (Safferstone, M., 2007). This is because most significant organisations in the eighteenth and nineteenth century were 'military' with strong hierarchical structure. In such frameworks leadership played a major role in creating stability and maintaining the status quo. Whilst the principles used were to manage conflicts, control crisis or even convince groups to acts as desired, the values and perceptions related with management and supervision were not clearly defined (Douglas, 2010). Therefore, many intellectuals argue that the old/traditional theories related to leadership and management may not suit contemporary organisational structures. Nevertheless, most traditional principles stress on common characteristics and behaviours that a leader possesses and his unique ability to control, direct and influence followers to desired outcomes (Gibney, 2009). On that note, Burns (1978) argues that the notion of leadership formed with emphasis on leaders' traits and personalities and these characteristics are still emphasised in contemporary organisations and cannot be overlooked.

The recent and more contemporary development of theories is mainly dominated by the 'managerial' theory of leadership, regarding how management practices can best be applied in achieving production. It focuses on interactive relationship between leaders and followers, and how mutual influence can lead to motivation and reaching common aims and objectives (Safferstone, M., 2007). With recent shifts in technology, generation and thinking, modern leadership emphasis is put on constant improvement in a complex and dynamic work environment. Employers ensure the comfort and satisfaction of their employees and continuously prepare themselves for dealing with change.

Table 1 – Differences between Traditional Leadership and Modern Leadership (Gibney *et al*, 2009)

Traditional Leadership	Modern Leadership
Presence of One function/one organisation	Presence of Cross-boundary
Hierarchical in nature	Collaborative/relational in nature
Linear type	Composite type
A specific problem/task taken in to consideration	Integrated vision of the task
Leader leverages personal networks during decision making	Brings together diverse networks during decision making
Time limited	Time extensive
Commitment to one cause/idea at one time	Holistic in process

Followers of traditional theories believe that the effective leader needs certain characteristics such as trust, inspiration, emotional intelligence and charisma, which can be applied in different scenarios such as business organisations, education platforms or war grounds. Their belief excludes the importance of situation and focuses mainly on leader's ability to set a vision and solve problems using his personal attributes (Sadler 1997). This proposal is a risky proposition at best due to rapid state of change and complex scenarios facing firms on daily basis. There are other loopholes identified in traditional approach of leadership. For instance, Rosener (1997) explains that qualities that were recognised in the past by researchers mostly involved male attributes and modern theories deliver more consideration to female leadership traits. However it can be argued that due to structure of organisations and that fact that men were mostly posited for top ranks, the traditional/male oriented approach is justified to some extent. However it is evident that traditional leadership on its own, as sole leadership style can be insufficient, given that leaders must follow distinctive approaches to unfamiliar challenges.

Hence as the time passed, researchers placed the emphasis on looking closer at situation dependent practice instead of focusing mainly on finding a solution to leadership by certain combination of qualities (Yukl, 1989). According to Wright (1996), leaders cannot use a same style in contrasting situations because the context will always play a major role. He further explains that effective leadership requires unique combinations in different situations. This put greater stress on situational leadership and some researchers took this path as the only effective way of leadership development while most others associated effective leaders with 'style' and their ability to shape or change it in different situations.

Hesay and Blanchar (1977) model of leadership identifies four key leadership styles for contrasting situations:

1. Telling (high task/low relationship behaviour)
2. Selling (high task/high relationship behaviour)
3. Participating (high relationship/low task behaviour)
4. Delegating (low relationship/low task behaviour)

Maturity Level	Most Appropriate Leadership Style
M1: Low maturity	S1: Telling/directing
M2: Medium maturity, limited skills	S2: Selling/coaching
M3: Medium maturity, higher skills	S3: Participating/supporting
M4: High maturity	S4: Delegating

The table above shows which leadership style is recommended leadership based on level maturity.

Leadership Style scenarios based on past personal observation and experience;

1. One of senior designers/head of design at 'Lawton Communication Group' in Southampton books an early holiday before Christmas. On her absence, another lead designer is in charge of her tasks who is familiar will all necessary procedures and responsibilities and he is excited for the upcoming challenge. Before her leave, she produces a list with full details and instructions of the upcoming tasks. It involves how the task must be carried out and also requests that nothing must be sent to clients before her approval through email.

    The result: The task is done efficiently but due to lack of trust, the relationship between the two colleagues is damaged. Although the other senior designer is 'M4', She uses 'S1' style of leadership instead of S4.

2. After working at Lawton communication group for 7 months, the junior designer is put in charge of producing in a magazine from concept to completion. As far as his line manager is concerned, the junior designer has gained enough experience and his fresh approach puts him in 'M3' maturity level. Therefore he uses S3 style of leadership and offers his support by daily discussions about progression and amendments where necessary. However, he leaves a large part of decision-making from concepts to style of design to his subordinate.

Result: Task is done successfully and the relationship between the colleagues is strengthened.

Caldwell & Rees (2011) argue that leaders must master their skills to make wise and well informed decisions to deal with ever increasing complexities in the contemporary business environment. This is due to dynamic nature of forces (e.g. political, economic, cultural, legal, etc.) surrounding the contemporary organisations and challenges they create for businesses today. In order to achieve production, building relationships between people is crucial in modern organisations. Unlike old approaches, new styles of leadership focus more towards 'participation' and emphasise on qualities of leaders influenced by situation and 'participation' of followers (Blanchard, et al., 1985). Researches noticed that this element not only improves productivity but also increases satisfaction among followers. From prior personal experiences and observations, this approach motivates subordinates to feel more motivated to tackle tasks with greater creativity and freedom. However, participation of subordinates put more emphasis on cultural factors in relation to 'situational theory'. According to Mouton and Blake's managerial grid model, culture plays a significant role on leader's power over their subordinates. They stress the importance of followers' characteristics as well as leaders' (Reddin, 1970).

Hofstede's research into national and organisational culture explains there are many different 'cultural factors', which deeply influence the ways people respond to different leadership styles. For instance in Asian culture the emphasis is put on 'collectivism' while the European culture values 'individualism'. This in return affects the way communication and style of leadership meets the followers' expectations. In addition to culture, there has been some emphasis put on 'gender'. Although leadership qualities in men (task-oriented) and women (caring, nurturing, delicate) may vary in terms of style but both are proven to be effective.

According to existing studies, women leaders are more effective in people-oriented sectors and men are more successful in task-oriented settings. Culture and gender also have a mutual relationship depending on the country of operation. Therefore, it is 'situation' that affects their style and creates contrast between them (Carothers, et al., 1999).

As is seen so far, what started as a mixture of personal traits (trait theory) transformed significantly over the period of time. Hue (2010) suggests that leadership has to be evaluated more carefully and move out of a strait jacket by combining elements that can provide a long lasting source of competitive advantage for organisations. To draw a line between values of traditional leadership and modern perspective, there are two popular approaches in contemporary literatures, which are 'transactional', and 'transformational' leadership styles (Burns, 1977). As mentioned earlier, in traditional style of leadership, the influences of a leader is passed on to subordinates with restricted contribution and collaboration on their part. Kuhnert and Lewis (1987), explain that transactional leadership is a more standard approach that can be associated with traditional style of leadership. Transactional leaders deal with their subordinates in a trade-like fashion and their rigid and strict fashion of leadership make their style unsuitable for contemporary organisational settings. Bass (1985) points out that transactional leaders acknowledge the purpose of work and are more focused on outcomes. They motivate their subordinates with rewards and promotions in exchange of their efforts. On the other hand Transformational leaders act as a 'change agent' and when faced with challenging problems, they envision positive outcomes and capitalise on opportunities. Transformational leaders create innovative and responsive solutions to navigate turbulent times and create a just, sustainable future for the organisation (Needle, D., 2004). In the context of Maslow's hierarchy of needs, transformational leaders are able to adjust and expand the subordinates' needs and wants. They aim to generate self-interest among subordinates to realise their full potential and subsequently develop them into future leaders. 'Kuczmarski, S. (2008) strongly argues that contemporary organisations today need a more collaborative approach than a commanding one and collaboration is a vital component of transformational leadership. She further explains that success of contemporary organisations depends on a leadership based on cooperation, inspiration, helping and serving others to maximise inner core potential and strengths. Only then the future growth and sustainability of the organisation is secured, because these additional strengths from the base builds the foundation of a successful business environment.

These days organisations are moving towards a more cohesive approach to standardise business culture and leadership styles and many argue that transformational leadership is the only effective style for contemporary organisations (Bass, 1994). However Maurik (2001) argues that due to higher level of uncertainty in demands along with challenges and complexities in contemporary organisations, transformational leaders face numerous problems. Since emotion and passion play a significant role in this approach, truth and reality are sometimes overlooked. For instance, transformational leadership does not consider situational dynamics where subordinates may not have the expertise or knowledge essential to complete a task or they are not motivated enough to implement without an immediate and substantial prize (Uncooperative followers). Transformational leadership is also time-consuming and leaders must invest energy to first convince and then get everyone on board to believe in a shared vision. Some organisations operate on achieving instant results and this approach will most likely create frustration and weaken organisational initial vision and goals (Goal Achievement) (Eagly, et al., 2003).

In the context of this study, the fish-bone diagram (Ishikawa, 1968) is used for problem solving / root cause analysis of concept design and quality defect prevention;

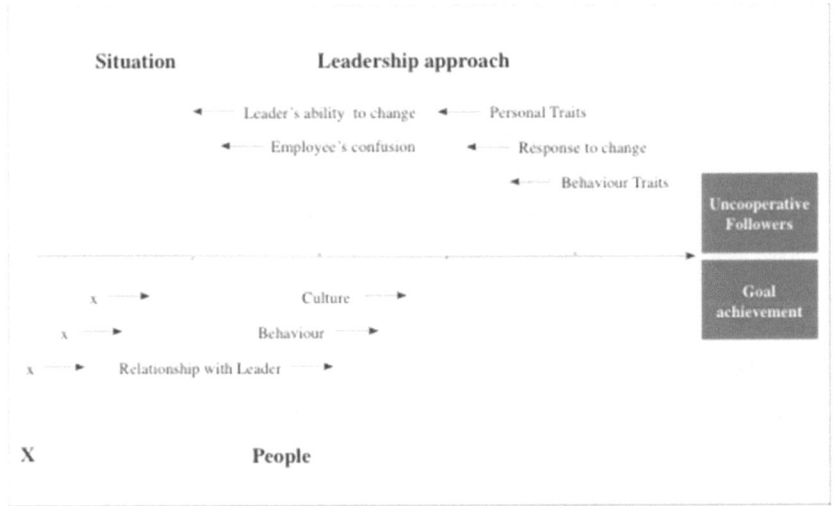

The diagram above identifies the possible effect or cause of the problem to be "**Uncooperative Followers**" (workforce in the business environment) and "**Goal achievement**". Moving backward, are possible factors contributing to the problem. In regards to transactional leadership / traditional leadership values, people and situation are perhaps eliminated and personally driven objectives are included. On the other hand, a transformational leader would place higher stress on people and diminish or eliminate the use of personal powers, which may lead to control loss in the long run. However, a situational leader will be more effective when it comes to responding to different needs. For instance if the need is collaboration among subordinates, he would put the emphasis on people and if the need is attaining certain goals, he would emphasise more on personal powers. The list of causes reveals that it is not possible to draw the full picture (of causes and effect) without both styles in play. Hence the solution will only be effective if all the factors mentioned are included. Furthermore recent studies also present some apparent dissimilarity of approaches in various geographical locations due to cultural differences. According to research, Americans follow a more transactional style of leadership with an authoritative approach. Their organisational structure shows stronger hierarchy and is more individualistic. On the other hand, Japan follows an opposite route, with more flexibility, collectivism and strong emphasis on job security (Aoki, K, et al., 2011). Evidence suggests that contradiction in culture results in different approaches in contemporary organisations and puts greater emphasis on the situational leadership approach.

It is only the situational leader that can emphasise on adaptability as a respond or build relationships and solve cultural issue that relate to people. The writer therefore concludes that 'situational leadership' as the most appropriate leadership approach in contemporary organisations. The flexibility in this style allows the leader to deal with ever changing and complex situations such as economic shifts, technological developments and rapid shifting global demands faced by contemporary organisations. This determines that there are no right (modern perspective) or wrong styles (traditional values), because the choice of style is continuously reviewed and suited for the particular situation of task and people.

In conclusion, there are three crucial factors identified in relation to an appropriate leadership style, which are as follows; structure or type of organisation, the situation it deals with, and the culture or the interaction of employees in the workplace. Contemporary leadership requires all action and modern organisations leadership programs must concentrate on cooperation, self-awareness, and expanding interpersonal relationships. This promotes two-way flow of knowledge, which leads to idea generation and further motivation. The disadvantage is leading to softer control system and diminished vision and objectives. However, The balance between traditional and contemporary style of leadership can fill the gap in both areas. For example, to increase efficiency, the authoritative and influencing characteristics that define traditional approaches can compensate for setbacks in contemporary approaches and create balance between goal orientation and human relations. On the other hand, higher effectiveness and productivity in contemporary organisations, which is achieved by establishing interpersonal relationships between leaders and followers, can improve traditional settings. Overall, as mentioned earlier, to create perfect balance between transactional and transformational interface, the situational leadership approach will add both flexibility and rigidity to meet organisational objectives.

To summarise, it is concluded that regardless of evolution of distinctive leadership theories developed over the years, a rightful balance is essential to maintain effectiveness. Today most businesses rely on leaders devotion, potentials and compassion to survive and strive in competition. Also setting a vision and objectives through planning and making sound and mindful decisions enables leaders to direct organisations towards achieving desired outcomes. Therefore, the traits mentioned above which finds its roots in traditional leadership is adopted in all organisations and cultures. However the effectiveness of these traits relies on their appropriate use to build stronger relationships among leaders and subordinates. As the gap tightens, collaboration becomes stronger and characteristics, which are highlighted in contemporary organisations, come to surface. Therefore, the old literature with emphasis on traits will always set the foundation and base of organisational leadership. However minimising risk associated with this style in the dynamic environment of business today, determines its survival in the long run.

References & Bibliography

Adair, J. (2004). The John Adair Handbook of Management and Leadership. Thorogood, London, pp. 23-29

Bass, B.M. (1990). From transactional to transformational leadership: learning to share the vision. Organizational Dynamics, 18(3), pp. 19-31.

Bass, B.M. & Avolio, B.J. (1994). Improving Organizational Effectiveness through Transformational Leadership, Salt City, NY, pp. 31-67

Bass, B. M. (1985) Leadership and Performance beyond Expectation, Free Press, New York.

Bennis, W. (1998) On Becoming a Leader, Arrow, London.

Blake, R. and Mouton, J. S. (1978), The New Managerial Grid, Houston TX, Gulf.

Blake, R., & Mouton, J. (1964). The Managerial Grid: The Key to Leadership Excellence. Houston: Gulf Publishing Co, pp. 11-29, 30-35.

Blanchard, Kenneth H., Patricia Zigarmi, and Drea Zigarmi (1985). Leadership and the One Minute Manager: Increasing Effectiveness through Situational Leadership. New York: Morrow,.

Bogdan, R. F. & Biklen, S. (1992). Eight common questions about qualitative research. In Qualitative research for education: An Introduction to theory and methods Boston: Allyn & Bacon, pp. 40-43

Bolman, L. G. and Deal, T. E. (1997) Reframing Organizations. Artistry, choice and leadership (2nd ed.), Jossey-Bass, San Francisco

Burns, J.M. (1978). Leadership. NY: Harper & Row, Publishers, pp. 17-30

Burns, J. M. (1978) Leadership, HarperCollins, New York

Caldwell, C., & Rees, T. (2011), Beyond Leadership: Deep Learning for Sustainable business, Lead, England.

Carothers, B. J., & Allen, J. B. (1999). Relationships of employment status, gender role, insult, and gender with use of influence tactics. Sex Roles, 41, 375–387.

Culp, G. & Smith, A. (1997). Six Steps to Effective Delegation. The Journal of Management in Engineering, pp 30-37.

Dojbak, D.H., Burton, R.M., Obel, B. & Lauridsen, J. (2008). How failure to align organizational climate and leadership style affects performance. Management Decision, 46(3), pp. 406-432.

Douglas, B. (2010). Leadership: The ghost at the trillion dollar crash. European Management Journal, 28(4), pp. 269-277.

Eagly, A. H., Johannesen-Schmidt, M. C., & Van Engen, M. L. (2003). Transformational, transactional, and laissez-faire leadership styles

Fiedler, F.E. (1967). A Theory of Leadership Effectiveness. New York: McGraw-Hill, pp. 15-40.

Fiedler, F. E. and Garcia, J. E. (1987) New Approaches to Effective Leadership, John Wiley, New York

Fiedler, F. E. (1997) 'Situational control and a dynamic theory of leadership' in K. Grint (ed.) (1997) Leadership. Classical, contemporary and critical approaches, Oxford University Press, Oxford.

Frank, W., Cole, M.S & Humphrey, R.H. (2011). Emotional Intelligence: Sine Qua Non of Leadership or Folderol. Academy of Management Perspectives, 25(1), pp. 45-59

Gardner, J. (1989) On Leadership, Free Press, New York

Gerth, H. H. and Mills, C. Wright (eds.) (1991) From Max Weber. Essays in Sociology, Routledge, London

Gibney, J, Copeland, S and Murie, A (2009). Toward a 'New' Strategic Leadership of Place for the Knowledge-Based Economy. doi: 10.1177/1742715008098307 Leadership February 2009 vol. 5 no. 1 5-23

Grint, K. (ed.) (1997) Leadership. Classical, contemporary and critical approaches, Oxford University Press, Oxford.

Heifetz, R. A. (1994) Leadership Without Easy Answers, Cambridge, MA: Belknap Press.

Hersey, P., & Blanchard, K. H., (1999). Leadership and the One Minute Manager, William M, pp 14-31

Hersey, P. (1984) The Situational Leader, Warner, New York.

Hersey, P. and Blanchard, K. H. (1977) The Management of Organizational Behaviour (3rd ed), Upper Saddle River, Prentice Hall, N.J.

Hersey, P., & Blanchard, K. H. (1977). The Management of Organizational Behaviour. Upper Saddle River N. J: Prentice Hall, pp. 14-28.

Hofstede, G. (2000). Culture's consequences: comparing values, behaviors, institutions, and organizations across nations. 2nd ed. Thousand Oaks: Sage Publications.

Huy, Q.N. (2010). Truth about Middle managers: Who They Are, How They Work, Why They Matter. Administrative Science Quarterly, 55(1), pp. 167-169

Huy, Q.N. (2001). In praise of Middle Managers. Harvard Business Review, September-October, pp. 72-79

Ishikawa, Kaoru (1968). Guide to Quality Control. Tokyo: JUSE

Jacobides, M. (2009) 'New thinking on how to do business', Financial Times, Managing in a Downturn Series, February 12. Available online from: http://www.ft.com/reports/managingdownturn Accessed 10 November 2013

Kiger, P (2005). With baby boomers graying, employers are urged to act now to avoid skill shortages. Workforce Management, 84(13), 52-54.

Kuczmarski, S. (2008), Changing the way we lead and succeed, AMA.

Kouzes, J. M. and Posner, B. Z. (1995) The Leadership Challenge, Jossey-Bass, San Francisco

Maurik, J. (2001) Writers on Leadership, Penguin, London.

McGregor, D. (1960) The Human Side of Enterprise, McGraw Hill, N.Y.

Mann, R. D. (1959) 'A review of the relationship between personality and performance in small groups', Psychological Bulletin 66(4), pp. 241-70.

Nanus, B. (1992) Visionary Leadership. Creating a compelling sense of direction for your organization, Jossey-Bass, San Francisco

Needle, D.(2004), Business in Context (4th ed.), Cengage Learning, UK, p. 248

Reddin, W. J. (1970) Managerial Effectiveness, McGraw Hill, N.Y.

Reddin, W. J. (1987) How to Make Management Style More Effective, McGraw Hill, Maidenhead

Rosener, J. B. 'Sexual static' in K. Grint (ed.) (1997) Leadership. Classical, contemporary and critical approaches, Oxford University Press, Oxford

Rossi, J (2007). What Generation Gap? Training and Development, 61(11), 10-11.

Sadler, P. (1997) Leadership, Kogan Page, London

Safferstone, M. (2007), Organizational Leadership: Classic Works and Contemporary Perspectives, University of Mary Washington, USA, Volume 5 (1)

Schwepker, C.H. & Good, D, J. (2010). Transformational Leadership and its Impact on Sales Force moral judgement. Journal of Personal selling and sales Management, 30(4), pp. 299-318.

Scott, D.S. & Ashford, S. J. (2010). Who will Lead and Who will follow? A Social process of leadership identity construction in organizations. Academy of Management Review, 35 (4), pp. 627-647

Senge, P. M. (1990) The Fifth Discipline. The art and practice of the learning organization, Random House, London

Stogdill, R. M. (1948) 'Personal factors associated with leadership. A survey of the literature, Journal of Psychology, Vol. 25, PP. 35-71.

Stogdill, R. M. (1974) Handbook of Leadership. A survey of theory and research, Free Press, N.Y.

Senge, P.M.(1990). The Leader's New Work: Building Learning Organizations. Sloan Management Review, pp. 7-33.

Selznick, P. (1957). Leadership in Administration: A Sociological Interpretation

Wright, P. (1996) Managerial Leadership, Routledge, London.

Yukl, G. (1989). Managerial leadership: a review of theory and research. Journal of Management, 15, 251-89

Zenger, J, Ulrich, D, & Smallwood, N (2000). The new leadership development. Training and Development, 54(3), 22-7

YOUR KNOWLEDGE HAS VALUE

- We will publish your bachelor's and master's thesis, essays and papers

- Your own eBook and book - sold worldwide in all relevant shops

- Earn money with each sale

Upload your text at www.GRIN.com
and publish for free